THE FIVE-MINUTE

FLOWER
ARRANGER

THE FIVE-MINUTE
FLOWER
ARRANGER

JANE NEWDICK

Text and illustration copyright © Breslich & Foss 1989

Published by Crown Publishers, Inc., 201 East 50th Street
New York, New York 10022

CROWN is a trademark of Crown Publishers, Inc.

Manufactured in Belgium

Library of Congress Cataloging-in-Publication Data

Newdick, Jane.
The five minute flower arranger / Jane Newdick.
p.   cm.
ISBN 0-517-57342-3
1. Flower arrangement.   2. Flower arrangement—Pictorial
works.   I. Title.
SB449.N36 1989
745.92'2—dc19   89–1336
CIP

ISBN 0-517-57342-3

10   9   8   7   6   5   4   3   2

First Edition

Conceived and produced by Breslich & Foss
Golden House, 28-31 Great Pulteney Street
London W1R 3DD

Designed by Lisa Tai
Typeset by Angel Graphics
Printed and bound in Belgium by Brepols

CONTENTS

THE FIVE-MINUTE APPROACH

Unless you positively enjoy the therapy of slowly building up a flower arrangement bit by bit and carefully adapting every branch and stem to fit precisely where you planned, you will find five minutes sufficient time for most arrangements. You may not finish up with a complicated Dutch master of a vase-full, but you will have something good to look at and a fresh idea.

Most people want flowers in their homes to cheer a room and to add color and scent as well as to provide the special quality that real blooms bring with them. A house without a living plant or pot of flowers is a sad place and does not possess a friendly, warm and lived-in atmosphere. Flowers do not have to be elaborately arranged in formal shapes and traditional designs to add sparkle and warmth to a room, and are better when they are allowed to speak for themselves in an uncomplicated way. In flower arranging the happiest results are often the simplest – the hastily assembled bunch of mixed flowers picked in a hurry from the garden and placed unceremoniously in a well used kitchen jug. The result may not be worthy of the word 'arrangement' but nonetheless has an honesty and immediacy which is often lacking in a formal approach.

Many people are scared to attempt even the simplest ideas with flowers because of their uncertainty about the 'rules', and this inhibits any natural skill or creativity they may have. The only skills needed for five-minute flower arrangements are a pleasure in handling and working with flowers and an enjoyment of experimenting a little and not minding if the first few attempts do not achieve the desired result.

Begin with arrangements which consist of just a container and a bunch of simple flowers. Make a posy in your hand, building up flower by flower and turning the bunch as you go. When you have a big enough posy trim the stems to the same length and stand the whole thing in the container. You may wish to loosen the blooms a little or may decide that the arrangement will look prettier if the heads are together.

Once you have more confidence you can begin to experiment with different kinds of containers and the types of flowers that you put together. The five-minute approach makes use of unlikely materials too: for example, when flowers are scarce or difficult to come by why not use bunches of fresh herbs from the greengrocer or a mixture of decorative fruit or vegetables with just a few fresh or dried blooms. Make use of abundant garden produce when it is available and, if you have access to a plot of land, try to grow a few easy flowers for cutting. Many of the ideas in the book can be adapted. You

Right Cut off all leaves and stems which will be below the water line in the container.

Center Cut stems on a long slant to expose maximum surface area.

Far right For bulb flowers, cut off any white part of the stem, leaving just the green.

can use different flowers from those suggested and, of course, in color schemes which you prefer or which fit in with a particular interior. Adapt and change where you wish – this book is certainly not about rules.

PREPARATION AND CONDITIONING

Whether your flowers have been picked from a garden or bought from a florist, it is worth spending a little time on preparing them before launching into your five-minute flower arrangement. You can of course use them straight away if you are in a hurry, and if they are florist flowers they may have been conditioned before you bought them. However, if you do not need to use them immediately, it is a good idea to let your flowers have a good long drink.

First of all, recut all the stems on a slant a little way up from their original cut. This will expose the maximum surface area of the stem to the water, allowing it to draw water up most efficiently. Also, some stems which have been cut for some time dry up and seal over. Woody stems like those of roses, lilac and many shrubs should be crushed, hammered or split a short way up the stem to allow them to absorb water more readily. A wooden mallet or rolling pin makes a good stem crusher but cutting the stem with sharp secateurs is probably the quickest way of dealing with tough stems.

Put flowers with newly-cut stems into a bucket or large jug with water which comes at least half way up their stems. Tepid or even warm water is best; avoid icy cold water straight from the cold tap. Roses can be left in their original wrap or can be rolled tightly in non-absorbent paper.

Left in a cool dark place for several hours or preferably overnight this water treatment will set flowers up for the next stage. You can either strip the stems of all their lower leaves and branches or simply cut the whole stem off for a low arrangement, depending on what you plan to do with your

Hammering the ends of woody stems helps them absorb water better.

Flowers that have not been conditioned should be given a long drink (up to 8 hours).

flowers. Some flowers, such as stocks and michaelmas daisies, turn the water quite smelly and unpleasant if bits of foliage are left to rot under water. A drop of household bleach can help to keep the water fresh and many bunches of flowers bought from a stall or florist come with a small sachet of a chemical designed to dissolve in the water and keep flowers fresh longer and the water sweet.

The water for your final arrangement is best at room temperature or slightly warm, not straight from the cold tap.

A few varieties of flower need slightly special treatment to last well. For example, poppies which at best have a brief life, need to have their stems either seared over a flame or dipped into boiling water for a couple of minutes. Euphorbias are another group of flowers which require this treatment and ranunculus also benefit from it. Foliage generally needs similar conditioning to flowers although tough leaves such as ivy are happy to be completely immersed in water for several hours which makes them last very well once they are fully

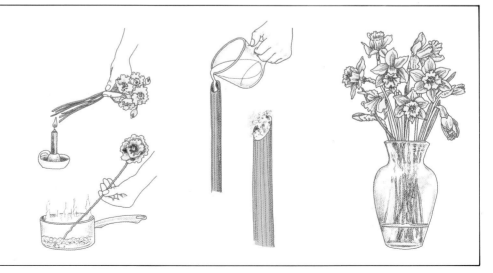

Right *To help poppies last longer, sear their ends over a flame (top), or use boiling water (bottom).*

Center *Large hollow stems can be filled with water and their ends plugged with cotton wool.*

Far right *Daffodils are easy flowers for the arranger. They need only a small amount of water and last a long time.*

charged with moisture.

If flowers collapse on you after they have been arranged, then it is worth trying to rescue them with a hot water treatment by re-cutting their stems and standing them in hot shallow water for about 15 minutes. They usually recover quickly ready to be put back in place.

CONTAINERS, MATERIALS AND TOOLS

A bunch of flowers is just a bunch of flowers until you add a container when, suddenly, it becomes an arrangement. Simply by standing that same bunch of flowers in a vase and spreading out the blooms you finish up with something special. The transformation has taken place by combining the two elements. Needless to say, the kind of container you choose is very important, whether the arrangement takes five minutes or half an hour.

In many cases it is not necessary to buy special vases as you can quite satisfactorily improvise with containers you already possess. Jugs make superb containers in any shape or size and so do kitchen storage jars and glass pots. Drinking glasses in simple straight shapes and more delicate stemmed wine glasses are fine for small flower arrangements. When you are faced with a large quantity of flowers try using a salad bowl or large kitchen mixing bowl.

Right *Simple items of kitchenware make ideal containers; such as a teapot or a jug.*

Far right *More unusual containers are old bottles, liqueur glasses or even a hollowed out melon.*

Right *Baskets of all shapes and sizes are very useful as containers.*

Far right *Smooth beach pebbles or clear or colored glass marbles can be used to weight heavy arrangements and hold stems.*

Baskets are useful for all types of flowers. Their color and texture make them especially suitable for simple groups. Make a small collection of pretty baskets and either use them lined with metal foil or plastic film and filled with a block of florist foam or simply stand a container within each one to hold the water.

A few simple glass tanks in varying sizes are perfect for five-minute arrangements. They always look elegant and under-stated and invariably make the best of whatever flowers you are using, even if there are only a very few stems. Tall cylindrical glass or plain colored ceramic pots are excellent for very long-stemmed flowers or branches that need only to be supported in water.

By their nature five-minute flower arrangements do not need many accessories to make them work. You may need a block or two of florist foam and perhaps a piece of crumpled wire netting to hold wayward stems in place. Sharp scissors or secateurs are vital tools and should be the best quality that you can afford. If you choose to work with scissors rather than secateurs, buy those which are designed specifically for florist work as they will be sharp enough to cut through tough stems but small and neat for working with delicate materials too.

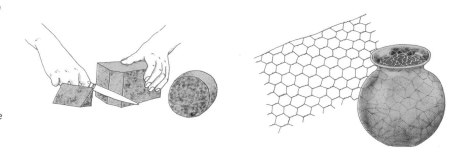

You will need rubber bands and/or string or wire for a few of the ideas in this book. Buy a small roll of fine wire designed for using with flowers and keep this together with scissors and foam in a safe place so you do not waste time needlessly every time you want to make an arrangement.

COLOR SCHEMES, SHAPES AND PROPORTIONS

Color is often the best starting point for an arrangement. You may want to put some flowers in a specific place in a room or on a dining table as a centerpiece for a special menu. The room's existing color scheme will suggest which flowers will work best. You may want to highlight a color that is already present or perhaps add a bolder brighter version of it to lift the room. Alternatively, you could aim for a complete contrast or even a totally outrageous effect.

One-color arrangements or graduated tones of one color can be successful but sometimes rather bland. If they are also the same color as the room itself there is the danger that the arrangement will simply melt away into the background. If you use a lot of one color in an arrangement add some relief in the form of plenty of green foliage.

All-white or cream flowers look sophisticated in any setting and are a good choice if there is any doubt as to what will look good in a certain setting; again, they need the contrast of some green to offset their pale blooms. Mixtures of strong colors often look spectacular together. A single dazzling color such as scarlet or golden yellow is the best choice to make for maximum impact.

Soft blues and mauves can look washed out and insignificant, but blue used with apricot or with yellow and white together looks fresh and unexpected. Pink and blue is another combination that always pleases. It is reminiscent of faded cotton prints, old china and herbaceous borders and has great charm.

Deciding the shape and proportion of a flower arrangement can daunt the first-time florist. Growers try to produce flowers with stems that are as long as possible. Long stems are fine for the few occasions when you want an enormous formal display but offputting and difficult when you want a more modest arrangement and have to cut the stems accordingly.

The container almost always dictates the height of the flowers you need as well as the shape and type of flower species. It is a good idea to bear in mind the container you plan to use before buying or picking the flowers. There will always be occasions though when you are given a bunch of flowers and then have to think of a way of using and displaying them. Simple glass containers really come into their own at such times.

Never be frightened of cutting stems short, making a bunch of flowers all the same height and just standing them in a low container. This is particularly appropriate for a low table or mealtime arrangement where it is desirable to keep lines of vision clear. Try to avoid top-heavy and clumsy arrangements with flowers that are too tall for their container. Conversely, do not use short stems in a tall vase that demands long stems. Try to aim for a proportion of flower to vase in which the flower is never less than a third taller or over two thirds taller than the vase.

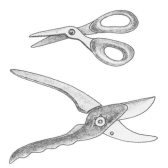

Tools for cutting and pruning: special florists' scissors or good quality secateurs.

It is important to get the right proportion of flowers to pot. Common mistakes are having flowers that are too short (left) or too tall (center) for their container. The illustration right shows the correct balance.

FINDING THE FLOWERS

The fortunate people who have access to a garden which produces flowers for picking have no problem finding flowers. For most of us, however, a visit to a flower shop or market stall is the first stage in a flower arrangement. Choose flowers with care and learn to look for signs which show that they are fresh and only recently arrived from the grower or wholesaler.

Many of the varieties of flowers for sale are grown commercially for their toughness and long life as cut blooms, others are more fragile and less likely to be long-lasting. Flowers should generally last at least 6 or 7 days in an arrangement.

Buy from a shop or stall which has a quick turnover and plenty of variety. Choose flowers with crisp foliage and blooms that are just out of the bud stage and not fully open. Many supermarkets and large stores have ready made up bunches of flowers as well as good quality unmixed varieties. They do not usually offer a wide choice and often only very ordinary everyday varieties, but it can be useful to pick up a bunch of flowers last minute with the shopping on the way home.

At one time flowers had specific seasons or times when they flowered and thus became available, with perhaps a few special varieties 'forced' or grown under glass. Nowadays it is possible to buy summer flowers all through the year, spring flowers in autumn and exotica flown in from all over the world. Out of season flowers though are generally still more expensive than outdoor or in-season blooms, so check before you buy a tempting bunch of sweetpeas in February. However, at certain times of the year it can be better value to buy foreign imported flowers than forced home-grown ones.

Flowers bought from a flower shop will generally have been prepared and conditioned before they are sold. If you buy from a street market or stall it is worth checking whether they have had any preparation or whether they have simply been stood in water straight from the packing box.

If you own a garden you will probably have produce available all-year round. Space permitting, it is certainly worthwhile to sow some annual flower seeds for a row or two of blooms especially for cutting. One packet of seeds of cornflowers, for example, will give you a bunch a day through the summer months. Many flowers provide blooms the more you pick them.

Good foliage is difficult to buy and well worth growing in a garden. Plant a shrub or two with variegated leaves and one or two other plants which have varied and interesting leaf shapes – these can lend an individual touch to an otherwise very ordinary bunch of flowers.

1
CITY CHIC

TULIPS AND GOLD PAPER

Ingredients
10 stems of apricot tulips
Large handful of cotton
  wool
Watertight plastic bag
Rubber band
Piece of gold paper or
  crumpled metal foil
Ribbon to tie bunch

This idea is perfect for anyone who feels too nervous to arrange flowers in a vase. Instead the flower stems are wrapped in damp wadding and sealed in a plastic bag before being wrapped in shiny gold foil to look as if the most elegantly wrapped bunch of flowers has just been put down casually for a few moments. This kind of arrangement really demands uncluttered and sophisticated surroundings as the point might be lost if it was put down on a surface already littered with bits and pieces.

Flowers wrapped in this way are best positioned on a low table or stool or on a wide window sill or bedside table and benefit from some subtle spotlighting. If the wadding round the stems is thick enough the flowers will be held just clear of the surface. If they seem rather squashed, cheat slightly by wedging something small under the foil to lift the flowers up.

Flowers treated in this way should last a few days although not quite as long as if they were in water – certain very long-lasting varieties, such as chincherinchees, chrysanthemum, pinks and alstroemeria, will be quite happy for several days. How long flowers last depends very much on room temperature and humidity and whether there is always water for the stems. As a preliminary step, be sure that the tulips have a good drink of water for several hours.

1 *Thoroughly soak cotton wool in water and wrap round tulip stems, covering them completely.*

2 *Put stems and wadding into plastic bag and secure with a rubber band where bag covers stems.*

3 *Wrap the paper or foil loosely round the lower stems, then tie the paper firmly in place with ribbon.*

FLOWERS IN A ROW

Ingredients

5 or more small
  containers such as small
  stemmed glasses. An
  odd number is visually
  more satisfying than an
  even number.
A flower head for each
  glass plus a few extra
  flowers.

A good way to make the most of a few flowers is to use single blooms in a row or group of containers. Small wine or liquer glasses are ideal containers as most people have a set of these. A group of glasses of the same shape and size look slick and sophisticated when placed in a well spaced row. Alternatively, you could use a selection of glasses of roughly the same volume but of different designs.

For a simple and more homely version, save small glass pots which have been used for jams or yogurt. The flowers used in this idea can be left-overs from a more elaborate arrangement or a few choice blooms bought or picked for their special appeal. A simple color scheme works best, and here the freshness of blue-edged glasses looks cool and elegant with sunny yellow and white. Try an all-pink version using flower heads in the pink to peach range, or keep all the flowers white and add one or two pieces of foliage.

Check the water level regularly and replenish often as the glasses are so small. A row of flowers will look at their best when situated close to eye level, so find a high shelf or mantelpiece for maximum impact.

1 *Cut each flower stem to the right height for your containers. Fill each glass with water and put a flower in each of them.*

2 *In one or two add an extra flower or little spray to fill out any which look small or unbalanced with the rest.*

PINK TULIPS IN A BUTTERFLY VASE

Ingredient
Large wide-necked vase
7 sprays of variegated
  euphorbia
15 stems of pale pink
  tulips (Angelique
  variety)
3 bushy sprays of pink
  genista

Tulips are usually best arranged alone to show off their good shape and habit of growth as they continue to open from bud stage and grow longer stems, moving and twisting towards a light source. These characteristics can make combining tulips with other flowers difficult. The semi double variety called Angelique is a very pretty mix of pink and white, with frilled and wavy petal edges. Angelique lasts and lasts in water, mixes happily with other flowers and foliage and is well behaved, opening out to reveal golden yellow stamens and center. The foliage is a soft greyish green which looks superb mixed with a variegated euphorbia. Although some tulip foliage is best stripped away, in this variety it is small-scale and a definite advantage to the arrangement.

The arching sprays of pale pink genista echo the habit of the curving tulip stems and add little points of darker pink all through the arrangement. Genista comes in several colors and is very useful as a mixer or filler in many flower arrangements. It also has a delicious scent.

1 *Prepare the flowers by making sure that you have removed any foliage below the water line.*

2 *Start the arrangement by putting sprays of euphorbia round the edge of the vase, spacing them out equally.*

3 *Add the the stems of tulip, spacing them evenly among the foliage and into the middle of the vase.*

4 *Add sprays of genista, splitting them into single stems if very bushy. Try to mix them throughout the arrangement.*

BLACK VASE AND GREEN APPLE

Ingredients
A classic curved vase
1 bamboo stem
3 iris leaves
1 stem of viburnum opulus
1 stem of rhubarb flower
1 acanthus leaf
5 parrot tulips
2 white ranunculus
1 green apple

Some of the most dramatic and successful flower arrangements rely on shape and silhouette for their appeal. For this kind of design it is perhaps more important to mix elements of strong outline, shape and texture with color as a secondary consideration. Look out for strap-shaped leaves and spiky grasses, interesting seed heads or flowers in bud.

The classic shape and uncompromising color of this small black vase need a dramatic statement either from boldly shaped materials or brilliant hues. Here the soft round shapes of many petaled ranunculus and balls of viburnum contrast with pointed blades of iris leaves and bamboo and the ragged frilled petal edges of parrot tulips.

The green apple picks up the green theme of the flowers and adds its own sculptural shape. Narrow-necked vases look very elegant but fitting everything into such a shape can prove difficult. Try to use naturally-arching flowers which curve away from the center and those with thinnish stems.

1 Assemble all the material and prepare stems, leaving just one or two tulip leaves on them.

2 Put rhubarb flower into vase and add viburnum opposite. Put bamboo leaf on one side and three iris leaves fanned out on other.

3 Stand acanthus leaf center back. Put all the tulips as a group leaning out of vase to balance rhubarb and viburnum.

4 Add the ranunculus to make a central focal point. Stand the vase in position and put the apple beside it.

HEIRLOOMS AND FLOWER HEADS

Ingredients

3 beautiful old containers
of china or glass

A mixture of flowers with
short stems, for
example:

Hippeastrums, iris,
carnations, roses,·
tulips, agapanthus,
lilies, alstroemeria,
anemones, guelder
rose, nerine

What you choose will
depend on the size,
shape and decoration of
your container.

Large flowers usually come on long stems which most people are loathe to cut. However, with shortened stems the flower heads look dramatically different and their beauty of form and detail are accentuated. If you hate to cut off stems wait until you have some flower heads which have dropped off or been severed from a main stem and then experiment using a few unlikely containers.

Old porcelain or glass are ideal containers for use in this way, with their wonderful colors and exquisite decoration. You can mix together quite startling colors and somehow the colors and designs of the cups and containers keep the overall effect within acceptable bounds. If you do not own containers in a variety of shapes and types, simply use a few tea or coffee cups; they can look very effective standing in a row along a shelf or mantelpiece.

Flowers that are perfect for this type of arrangement include various lilies and orchids, hippeastrum, alstroemeria, iris, hellebore, peonies and roses.

1 *Choose 3 containers, either cups, jugs or sugar bowls of similar size which are prettily patterned.*

2 *Prepare the flowers by cutting the stems short to fit the cups. Strip away any unnecessary foliage and leaves.*

3 *Fill the cups with water and build up arrangement flower by flower, contrasting colors where possible for greater impact.*

4 *Arrange the three containers in a pleasing fashion on a shelf or mantelpiece for greatest impact.*

WHITE LILIES AND SMOOTH PEBBLES

Ingredients

A rectangular glass tank
8 or more smooth beach
  pebbles
A smaller square glass
  tank
6 or more small smooth
  beach pebbles
4 stems of white
  longiflorum lilies
2 stems of artichoke
  foliage or similar leaves
A small bunch of white
  single daisies or
  chrysanthemums

Plain rectangular glass tanks are very useful containers for both simple and sophisticated arrangements. They look superb packed densely with flowers of a single variety or holding one or two carefully chosen stems.

While shapely stems look good when viewed through glass there is also room for additional visual interest in the form of pebbles, glass or colored marbles. Pebbles seen underwater display colors that are not obvious when they are dry and add a hint of beach and seascape or pond and water garden. Use the pebbles to anchor wayward stems and to keep the center of gravity low on top-heavy arrangements.

Do not allow the water inside the tank to become stale and cloudy; change it entirely if you need to and wash the pebbles each time. A tiny piece of charcoal will keep the water fresh and the flowers happy; using an additive to prolong flower life will make the water murky and unattractive.

White longiflorum lilies are long-lasting and have a beautiful scent. Each bud opens out slowly and the lower ones can be removed as they fade.

1 *Prepare flowers by removing foliage from lower stems. Fill tanks with water and carefully put pebbles on bottom.*

2 *Lodge the 2 foliage stems on one side of large tank, using the pebbles to anchor the stems in place.*

3 *Add lily blooms on other side. Put small daisies in square tank and stand it beside the larger one.*

2
SCULPTURAL
SIMPLICITY

GLASS TANK AND GLADIOLI

Ingredients
10 stems of white bridal
   gladioli
1 stem of variegated ivy
2 leaves of *Helleborus
   corsicus*
1 spray of vine leaves
An oblong glass tank

A glass tank is one of the most useful containers for making very quick simple arrangements. Any flowers and foliage put into a glass shape take on a very different look from those placed in a solid ceramic vase. The stems beneath the water are as important visually as the flowers above, so bear this in mind when preparing the flowers. Make sure the stems are clean and without leaves, which will rot and spoil the water. Flowers put into this type of container will usually fall naturally into a good shape. However, they will look best if all the stems are roughly the same length. There are two basic approaches when using a glass tank. Either fill the container very full with flowers such as tulips, daffodils or anemones, or as here use very few stems and allow the spaces between the flowers to be as important as the blooms themselves.

Position the filled tank with a light source, such as a window, behind it or to one side to ensure maximum sparkle and reflection through the glass. Placing the tank on a shiny surface will produce even more interesting effects as one material meets another.

1 *Prepare stems and foliage. Put foliage into tank and space it out. Balance this with foliage on the opposite side.*

2 *Place hellebore leaves against back and front of tank. Put gladioli among the foliage.*

RANUNCULUS AND FROSTED GLASSES

Ingredients

A pair of trumpet-shaped
  glasses
16 stems of ranunculus

There is more to choosing a container for an arrangement than simply suiting the size or style of flowers which you intend to use. The shape of a vase or whatever container you want to use will often dictate the final look of the arrangement.

A trumpet shaped glass (see illustration) will simply encourage the flower stems to spread into a fan shape with very little help from you. A container or two of this shape and size is useful for any medium-sized flower with stiff stems, such as ranunculus, roses, anemones, freesias, pinks and miniature gladioli. Many classic vase shapes are narrow at the bottom and widen out to the top. Some are flattened from front to back and produce an even more stylized fan-shape of flowers.

These pale green frosted dessert glasses work beautifully as flower containers; two used together will produce a mirror-image effect. Flowers arranged in this way look best with plenty of space and air round each stem rather than being bunched closely together.

1 *Clean and split the ranunculus first. Trim away any leaves and cut off small flower buds to make single clean stems.*

2 *Measure all the stems against the height of the glass to determine where to cut.*

3 *Fill the glasses with water, bunch the flowers in your hand and trim evenly.*

4 *Put them into the glass and let them fall outwards to the rim of the glass. The buds will open a few days later.*

HIPPEASTRUMS AND GLASS CYLINDERS

Ingredients

2 narrow heavy glass
cylinders, one shorter
than the other
2 stems of apricot
hippeastrum
2 rubber bands
Cotton wool (optional)

A flower as stately as hippeastrum (sometimes known as amaryllis) needs little attention to make the most of its potential. A tall thick glass cylinder is perfect to take the weight and height of a flower like this and it is definitely a shame to cut off much stem, unless you use the flower head alone. To help the stem take up moisture, fill with water and plug the hollow end with a small piece of cotton wool; this makes the end very fragile so secure it with a rubber band to prevent it splitting and ruining the stem. If you do not like the look of a rubber band you can use fine wool, cotton thread or natural raffia instead.

Hippeastrum come in several colors ranging from cool greeny whites, pale apricot shades, rich burnt orange-reds, and very pretty blush pinks and whites reminiscent of apple blossom.

1 Trim one stem of hippeastrum roughly 2 inches (5 cm) shorter than the other and split both

2 Measure the flower stems against the cylinders and decide on the right height. Cut off excess, if necessary.

3 Secure end of stem with rubber band. If you want to – fill stems with water.

4 Plug end with scrap of cotton wool and stand the stems in the cylinders, half filled with water.

CHINESE BASKETS AND ARTICHOKES

Ingredients

1 basket approx. 6 inches (14 cm) square
1 basket approx. 5 inches (11 cm) square
Florist foam
Metal foil or plastic wrap
4 artichokes
2 large flower heads, such as hippeastrum, with 2½ inch (5 cm) stems
6 or 7 sprays of lilac or similar shrub blossom with 2½ inch (5 cm) stems
1 bunch of bear grass

Arrangements using large and simple ingredients are often easier for a beginner to achieve than those using long-stemmed flowers in a freer way. In this kind of basket arrangement there are only a few choices of position for each ingredient.

When artichokes are plentiful use them to make beautiful sculptural arrangements. If you grow them yourself, leave some until the flowering stage when the centers open to reveal brilliant purple-blue tufts of petals. To balance the powerful shapes of the artichokes choose flowers which are equally bold, such as large lily heads, camellias, hippeastrums or hemerocallis, or any flower with a strong outline and striking color. The bear grass used in one basket is normally bought fresh or you can dry it to use over and over again. More commonly seen used in a bunch to spill out from an arrangement, it looks splendid twisted and wrapped to add definition and shape among flowers. Using two containers of different sizes together makes a very satisfying arrangement – where one small container might look lost, two together make a bolder statement.

1 Cut foam to fit basket. Line basket with foil or wrap and put wet foam in place. Secure one end of bear grass with rubber band.

2 Wrap hank of grass inside large basket. Add one artichoke to small basket and three to large basket.

3 Put two flower heads diagonally into small basket and fill spaces in both baskets with sprays of lilac.

Pinks and Mauves in a Tank

Ingredients

A clear glass tank,
  rectangular
1 stem of mauve
  Singapore orchid
2 stems of small-leaved
  eucalyptus
1 stem of lilac
6-8 mauve and pink
  chrysanthemum flower
  heads
4 stems of mauve freesia

A pink and mauve color scheme can look very soft and pretty in a white, gray or pale pink interior, but it is quite difficult to work with successfully. There are plenty of flowers to choose from in these shades. The trick is to use pinks that have plenty of blue in their makeup and avoid peachy pinks as they add the wrong note of yellow to the color range.

Any foliage used with pinks and mauves is pretty in a bluish gray-green rather than an acid yellowish green. An arrangement of this type is very economical with flowers and looks best standing where it can benefit from strong side lighting to give sparkle to the water and glass. A glass container standing on glass gives interesting reflections and the illusion that the flowers are floating in space. Be sure that the stems showing beneath the water are clean and neat as they are an important visual element in this type of arrangement; any small leaves and stems left on will quickly rot and turn the water cloudy.

If properly prepared, all the flowers and foliage used in this arrangement should stay looking good for at least a week.

1 *If not done already, prepare all flower stems by stripping away small leaves and stems. Cut all stems to roughly the same height.*

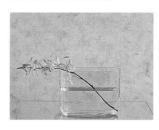

2 *Put the orchid in first, leaning it in place so that it curves gracefully over the side of the tank.*

3 *Put the eucalyptus beside it. Put lilac spray at back in the middle of the vase and add the chrysanthemums in a bunch at the front.*

4 *Finally, put freesia stems at other side, leaning in opposite direction to the orchid.*

ANEMONE TREE WITH GREEN MOSS

Ingredients

20 blooms of mixed anemones on long stems

A small cylinder of florist foam (standard size)

A strip of ribbon to wrap round foam block

Metal foil

A few pieces of fresh bun moss

A length of black cord or string

Rubber bands

The beautiful straight sturdy stems of anemones, their color and texture should be made the most of in arrangements. Here, a long-stemmed bunch has been decoratively tied with black cord and stood in a small block of wet florist foam. The black cord perfectly highlights the inky black centers of the flowers and the green moss and ribbon blends with the green frill round each flower head.

Anemones can be bought in bunches of mixed colors, as here, or in single colors. Choose a mixed bunch for this idea as it has more punch and contrast. This arrangement might appear complicated at first glance but it is very quick to put together. The flowers need only to have their ends trimmed neatly across. The foam block was bought ready-cut to this shape and size and needs only to be soaked in water.

Remember to cut a circle of foil to stand the foam on, to protect furniture from the dampnesss, or simply stand the whole thing on a small mat or saucer. Moss can be bought from most flower shops. Alternatively you can find your own, on tree roots and shady banks. This type of bun moss comes in small rounded tussocks and has just the right kind of effect for the anemone tree. To keep the flowers fresh, remove the moss occasionally and spray or pour extra water onto the foam; the flowers will use it up quite quickly from such a small source.

1 *Bunch anemones. Hold in place with rubber bands high up under flowers and at bottom of stems.*

2 *Soak foam and cut hole to accommodate stems. Wrap foil round foam and cut circle to stand foam on.*

3 *Pin ribbon round side of foam. Stand flowers in foam. Cover top of foam with moss.*

3
COUNTRY
CHARACTER

MARIGOLDS AND MANDARINS

Ingredients
A glazed earthenware
  storage jar or jug
10 stems of marigolds
A basket of small
  mandarin oranges

Marigolds speak for themselves through their simple shape and bright color. They are not the kind of flowers which work well mixed into more formal arrangements and their bright, almost brash, shade of orange is difficult to use with other flowers. It is best to find a sturdy, sympathetic container such as an earthenware crock or jar and simply bunch the marigolds inside. Marigolds need no special treatment and last well as cut flowers.

If you are able to buy or pick tall, strong marigolds the arrangement can be stood on the floor. Caught in a ray of light, marigolds bring a sunny, Mediterranean feel to any room however dark and gloomy it is.

Flowers which have very strong colors need the foil of fresh greenery, so either add extra foliage to the arrangement or keep plenty of leaves on the flower stems. The sharp fresh green of the marigold leaves tones down the vibrant orange of the flower heads.

1 *Trim the ends of marigolds but leave all the leaves on except those below the water. Make a bunch in your hand and stand in the jar.*

2 *Choose containers with a robust character and an earthiness to contrast with the vivid color of the flowers and oranges.*

HYACINTH GLASSES AND GARDEN FLOWERS

Ingredients
Colored glass hyacinth pots
A selection of small leaves and flowers
Hellebore corsicus, pulmonaria, hyacinth, rue, winter honeysuckle, tellima grandiflora purpurea, viburnum tinus.
Rubber bands, fine rose wire or string

Hyacinth glasses make lovely containers for flowers but usually get forgotten once the hyacinths are finished. Small rounded bunches of miniature flowers look very pretty sitting in the top curve of the glass with their stems showing in the lower part of the glass.

Most gardens can provide a few snippets of flowers and leaves to make into a tiny bouquet. Choose leaves which have interesting colors and shapes and add just a few stems of flowers, especially scented ones if you have them. Tie the bunches before dropping them into the glasses. The end result is neat and pretty and achieved with a minimum of time and effort.

This is a useful method for any arrangement which is going to be seen in the round, and is just as suitable for a large bunch of tall flowers as it is for miniature posies. To copy this idea with bought flowers, simply choose small sprigs or sprays which can be broken down into smaller parts.

1 *Choose flowers for each bunch, mixing them well. If need be make small sprigs from larger stems.*

2 *Make small bunches in the hand, adding a stem or two at a time. Vary the colors as you work round the bunch.*

3 *When the bunch is big enough, secure with a rubber band, fine rose wire or some string.*

4 *Trim the ends of the bunches neatly and place in hyacinth jars which have been filled with water to cover the stems.*

APRICOT AND PEACH WITH TERRACOTTA POT

Ingredients

A glass container
A terracotta flower pot and saucer
3 stems of apricot lilies
2 stems of apricot 'hippeastrum
1 stem of orange lily
2 stems of yellow alstroemeria
1 stem apricot spray chrysanthemum
1 stem of apricot spray carnation
3 stems of apricot genista
2 stems of solidago ('golden rod')

A terracotta flower pot may not appear to be an obvious first choice as a container for cut flowers, but its color works well with many different types of flowers. Most flower pots have drainage holes at the bottom, are unglazed and therefore not waterproof, so you will need to stand the arrangement inside a waterproof container which fits inside the clay pot.

A mixed arrangement of one basic color often only needs a splash of another color to bring it to life. Here the warm and gentle apricot and peach colors are made more intense by the addition of a small amount of golden yellow. Another way of enhancing these peachy colors is by mixing them with their contrasting color of greenish gray-blue. Eucalyptus leaves, for example, look good with all shades of apricot and peach.

This type of arrangement relies on being open and airy. Choose flowers with good outline shapes, some quite strong such as lilies and some softer flowers such as genista and solidago ('golden rod').

1 *Fill the glass container with water and stand it inside the terracotta pot, which has been placed on its saucer.*

2 *Trim flower stems, removing any leaves which will rest beneath waterline. Add stems one at a time mixing varieties as you go.*

3 *Keeping stems roughly the same height, continue placing flowers around the perimeter of the pot.*

4 *Any taller stems should stand in the middle, supported by the stems around the edge of the pot.*

LEMON, GREEN AND WHITE JUG

Ingredients

A large narrow jug
A piece of wire netting
5 stems of white larkspur
3 stems of molucella
3 stems of white allium
2 stems of white daisy
   spray chrysanthemum
4 stems of feverfew
3 stems of yellow roses
8 stems of white freesia
1 stem of yellow lily
1 stem of white lily
4 stems of yellow or white
   ranunculus
1 stem yellow alstroemeria

A large plain jug demands bold crisp flowers. To fill a container of this size you will need long-stemmed flowers which are left uncut.

This arrangement is designed to be viewed from one side, so the tallest stems are put at the back of the jug to fan out and make a framework. The weight of the jug filled with water should anchor the whole arrangement. Even so it is probably a wise precaution to stand it near or against a wall. Pale colors like these are thrown into relief beautifully against a deep-colored background. Most of the flowers used in this arrangement are long-lasting and therefore economical. As the flowers age and wilt, remove them or add a few new fresh ones. Even with all the yellow flowers removed this group would still look pretty and fresh in white and green.

1 Crumple wire netting and put into neck of jug, hooking a cut end over edge to hold in place.

2 Trim and recut ends of stems, leaving them as long as possible.

3 Stand stems of larkspur and molucella at back of jug, in a fan shape. Spread white flowers throughout.

4 Add yellow flowers to balance the color, then alliums equally spaced throughout the arrangement.

PINK AND BLUE COUNTRY JUG

Ingredients

A mixture of cottage
garden flowers such as
poppies, roses,
larkspur, love-in-a-mist,
hydrangea, chive
flowers, asters, borage,
lavender, poppy seed
heads.

A jug

The containers you have will suggest ideas and color schemes for arrangements as well as the right choice of flower. This strongly patterned antique jug works beautifully with all shades of pink, blue, mauve and green but would fight with stark shapes or strong bold colors. A wide range of different garden flowers has been used here but all are softly colored and have quite fussy and detailed outlines. Packed closely together they look like the herbaceous border they originally came from. To avoid a messy result, make small bunches of each variety of flower first and then build up the arrangement bunch by bunch, putting one color beside a different one to get a rich texture. Try to see this dense kind of arrangement as patterned blocks of color and texture rather than individual flower heads and shapes.

The silhouette should make a curve and be about a third to a half as high as the container. Aim to make the result look good from all angles so that you can stand the jug in the middle of a table if you wish.

1 Put each type of flower variety into small bunches by color.

2 Strip off lower leaves for each bunch and cut ends of stems to one length.

3 Put shortest stemmed bunches at front and round edge of jug.

4 Put taller bunches at back and middle of jug. Mix colors thoroughly throughout.

Spring flowers and kitchen jars

Ingredients

2 tin storage jars or
 similar kitchen
 containers
For each jar:
6 stems of blue hyacinth
3 stems of mimosa
4 small pieces of white
 feverfew
3 stems of yellow genista
 (can be split if bunches
 are very large)
6 stems of yellow fennel
 flowers
3 or 4 yellow ranunculus

Using two containers, matching or otherwise, adds a whole new dimension to flower-arranging. You can stand them together and treat them as if they were part of one large arrangement, fill them separately but stand them side by side, or use them well away from each other, for example at opposite ends of a table or shelf.

If you do not possess many vases the first place to search for a substitute is in the kitchen. Plain shiny metal pans, molds and cake tins look superb filled with flowers and the solid shapes of jugs, mortars and salad bowls always compliment flowers.

This arrangement uses two old tin storage jars in a pale blue on white enamel design and carries on the kitchen theme, although it would look at home in any room in the house. There are many spring flowers in this color range and for later in the year it is possible to use blue larkspur or delphiniums, yellow daisies or coreopsis, achillea or solidago ('golden rod').

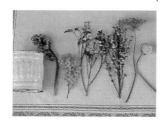

1 *Prepare flowers, removing leaves below waterline, split large bunches and count number of flowers for each jar.*

2 *Put hyacinths in jar first, leaning them against the rim. Add mimosa just inside the hyacinths.*

3 *Fill center of jar with stems of genista, then add feverfew and fennel throughout arrangement.*

4 *To finish, spot the ranunculus throughout the arrangement, and place both jars together where they will be displayed.*

4
TIMELESS
TEXTURE

Summer basket on a bookshelf

Ingredients

A shallow oval basket
A standard block of florist
    foam
Plastic film
8 to 10 stems of lilac
4 or 5 sprays of
    chrysanthemums
Bunch of white and pink
    anemones
10 small roses
10 ranunculus
5 freesias

This densely-packed basket of flowers looks complicated because many stems of several different varieties were used. To make this kind of arrangement work, have plenty of material to hand and build up a mass of texture, leaving few spaces between the blooms and allowing no flower to stand out higher than its neighbor either side. The whole arrangement curves gently with stems taller at the back than at the front, so you must work with this overall shape in mind, cutting stems as you go and keeping a smooth line. The basket is designed to be seen from the front, so the back can be quite flat.

The constrast of pale colors mixed with strong colors looks fine here because there is such an abundance of material and even the stronger colors have some white in their make-up. Though of different varieties, most of the flowers are the same simple round shape. The looser, larger areas of lilac are used as a filler, merging one flower with another.

Choose an oval basket that is fairly shallow but deep enough to hide a generous thickness of foam.

1 *Line basket with film, wet foam and put inside basket. Split chrysanthemum sprays into single-flower stems and hammer or split lilac twigs.*

2 *Fill basket with lilac. Make the back layer tallest, graduating down to front edge. Insert chrysanth-emums graduating again.*

3 *Add anemones, ranunculus and freesias evenly throughout basket, following the same plane.*

4 *Finally, add roses, balancing colors throughout and concentrating them at bottom front edge.*

DAFFODILS IN A BASKET NEST

Ingredients

A round nest basket
Water container to fit
   inside basket
Wire netting
40 mixed daffodils of at
   least 3 species
10 hazel catkin twigs

Shallow baskets are useful for dense, textural arrangements where a mass of color and detail is more important than shape and silhouette. It is possible to buy twig baskets woven with moss or you can add the moss yourself round the top of a plain basket. Alternatively, you can use the moss to fill the gaps between the flowers and the container. This arrangement is designed to look as natural as possible and uses several different types of daffodil and narcissi together to relieve what otherwise might be too much plain color.

The twigs and hazel catkins look pretty and spring-like but they are also useful in that they make a bed for the flower heads. A piece of wire netting has been put over the inner container to provide a framework for the many flowers being used. (Netting is often used by flower arrangers, in the neck of a jug or across a vase to help support heavy or thick stems.)

You can either buy proper plastic-coated netting for this purpose or simply cut a piece of old wire netting. Sometimes it is necessary to tape the wire into place but usually it can just be wedged firmly into position.

1 Cut all stems of twigs and daffodils to right height for basket. Fill inner container with water. Cut wire netting to fit over container.

2 Put container inside basket and tuck extra wire over edges into basket. Put twigs in, spacing them all over container.

3 Add small groups of daffodils throughout basket, using twigs as a framework.

4 Mix the three types and colors of daffodils and continue to fill the basket.

Hellebore blooms in goblets

Ingredients

1 or 2 large stemmed
goblets or similar
containers
8 large stems of
Hellebore corsicus and
Hellebore orientalis for
each container
Crumpled wire netting for
each container

To show off something as glamorous as these golden containers the flowers inside should look rich, old-fashioned and slightly understated.

The rich yet mellow colors of *Helleborus orientalis* and *H. corsicus* range from creamy green to deep maroon with some flowers having deeper colored freckles on the insides of their petals. Their stems are thick and sturdy and in an arrangement such as this are supported by crumpled wire mesh in the top of the container.

A few of the plants' smaller leaves are mixed with the flower heads to give a relaxed and natural feel.

Searing the ends of the hellerbores' stems over a flame seals them and should make the flower last much longer in water.

1 *Prepare the hellebore stems by removing lower leaves and searing ends over a flame.*

2 *Crumple wire netting to fit inside top edge of container. Add flowers, mixing colors and working round edge of the goblet.*

3 *Fill in the middle area and check from the final viewpoint that the overall shape is pleasing.*

PINK POSIES AND BLUE GLASSES

Ingredients

2 matching round
containers

10 stems of small pink
roses

10 pink cornflowers

10 stems of pink statice
(fresh not dried)

Enough pink spray
carnations to have 15
open flower heads

A pair of pink posies in pretty bubble glass would make a delightful arrangement for a low bedside table. The pinkness of the flowers is subtly counteracted by the cool blue of the glass. Once again, two look stunning where one might be insignificant. Using a pair of containers gives you the chance to play around with the contents, mixing and matching materials and having fun juxtaposing textures and different shades of pink. There is virtually no green in this idea to contrast with the petals. Instead, there is pure texture and plenty of scent. This is an arrangement for summer when roses are plentiful and annuals such as statice and cornflowers are freely available.

Flowers with their stems cut short and packed closely together possess great charm. This is a lovely way to present flowers you can obtain in abundance, whether they are spring daffodils or summer roses.

You could try a similar version using all yellow or blue flowers or peachy pinks and salmons. This type of arrangement is one of the simplest to put together and the flowers mentioned may well last several days.

1 Fill containers with water and select flower types for each container: roses and cornflowers for one, statice and carnations for the other.

2 Put roses in one glass and statice in the other, cutting stems to make flowers double the height of glass.

3 Continue filling one bowl completely with roses, and the other with the statice.

4 Next, add cornflowers to roses and carnations to statice, spreading evenly throughout.

FOLIAGE AND TWIGS IN AN ANTIQUE BASKET

Ingredients

A small basket with handle; an oval shape if possible

A selection of leaves and twigs, including evergreen and variegated ones. Bare colored stems such as cornus and rue, rosemary and cyclamen leaves. Choose some tall slender shapes and some lower bushier ones.

A standard block of florist foam

Plastic film

One of the real pleasures of growing plants in a garden is to be able to pick all kinds of twigs and foliage for simple arrangements throughout the year. Most gardens can provide some color and interest whatever the season. You may find various shades of green and brown appealing. Try to combine plain green leaves with a few which are variegated with cream or silvery white. Make use too of some of the less common herbs like rue and rosemary.

In the summer months it would be lovely to make a basket of different herbs each with a different scent, leaf shape and color. In mid-winter try using all evergreens and perhaps a few bare twigs with warm colors, such as cornus and willow, or leafless branches with clusters of berries.

Small baskets are perfect for many different types of flower arrangements. They can always be lined with metal foil or plastic film and used with florist foam, or they can be a decorative container for a waterproof vessel standing inside them.

1 First prepare the basket by lining with a double thickness of plastic film. Cut the florist foam and soak according to the maker's instructions.

2 Place foam in basket. Prepare the stems by splitting or hammering, as necessary, and then begin to fill the basket.

3 Work across the basket from side to side. Make small groups of one type of foliage, following the shape and curve of the handle.

4 Start with the back layer and work forwards, finishing with small stemmed decorative material such as the cyclamen leaves.

ROSES AND RANUNCULUS, ANEMONES AND RIBBON

Ingredients
3 lengths of ribbon to
match different flower
colors
3 small baskets of same
size and shape
Plastic film
Florist foam
12 to 15 flower heads per
basket. Choose from
roses, ranunculus,
anemones, tulips. In our
version one basket had
all anemones. One
basket had roses and
tulips mixed and the
third had pink and red
mixed ranunculus.

Three very small baskets are filled with a dense
pattern of petals in warm pink and red and finished
off with threaded ribbons to emphasize the effect.
Look out for tiny baskets that can be treated in this
way and have a loose enough weave to thread a ribbon
through. The baskets shown here are not quite round,
not quite square and each one is lined with plastic
film and wedged with florist foam. The simplest way
to arrange roses, ranunculus or anemones is to work
from above and simply place them in rows. You can
alternate flowers of different types and make colored
rows or a checkerboard effect, or you can try rings of
different colors or a random mix. Choose flowers that
are all roughly the same size and shape, and look for
contrasting petal textures and pretty centers for when
the flowers are fully open. Stand the finished group
on a dining table or on a low table near seating so that
it can be enjoyed at its best, from quite close up.

Be bold with the color mixing and use pale pinks
with vivid reds. Leave the ribbon ends simple and
preferably without a bow, which might make the
arrangements look too fussy.

1 *Thread ribbon through
basket slots and tie at front.
Line basket with double
thickness of plastic film.*

2 *Put soaked foam into
basket. Arrange flowers in
rows, working from one side
to the other.*

3 *Complete all the rows.
Alternate the roses and tulips
in one basket.*

5
JUST FOR
FUN

POPPIES AND BOWS

Ingredients
A large glass vase
A length of ribbon in main
    color, 2 inches (5 cm)
    wide
A length of ribbon in
    second color, 1 inch (2
    cm) wide
Dressmakers' pins
25-30 stems of Iceland
    poppies

The addition of some ribbon or a bow can transform a plain glass vase. Iceland poppies have a crumpled texture and translucency that is very similar to fabric. Adding a double bow to a vase of these flowers will emphasize the qualities of both petals and ribbon.

Avoid the type of ribbon normally sold for florist work and use proper dressmakers' ribbon. This shape of vase is perfect for ribbon treatment as it has a groove just below the top edge round which the first length of ribbon can be tied. On containers of a different shape the ribbon can be tied lower down or simply attached as a bow with a small patch of double-sided sticky tape. Iceland poppies are fragile to handle but last quite well as cut flowers, particularly if their stems are seared over a naked flame for a few seconds or stood in about 1 inch (2 cm) of boiling water for about a minute. Annual Shirley poppies are a good alternative to Iceland poppies. They are easy to grow, are available in pinks, reds and whites, and need the same stem treatment as suggested for Iceland poppies.

1 *Cut poppy stems and treat as described above. Put them in vase full of water, spreading the flowers evenly.*

2 *Take second color ribbon and make a bow.*

3 *Tie main color ribbon round neck of vase and make a bow at front*

4 *Pin second bow through center on to middle of first bow.*

DAFFODILS AND TWISTED TWIGS

Ingredients
A jug or container
3 or 4 stems of corkscrew
    hazel
15 daffodils

When the first bunches of daffodils appear for sale in late winter it is hard to resist their cheerful bloom. Notoriously difficult to mix with other flowers, they are best given simple treatment. Several bunches put together and with stems cut short look good when placed in a plain glass tank or low container and viewed from above. Daffodils always look right used with bare twigs, especially hazel. Freshly cut twigs will eventually open out into fresh green leaf. The jug used here as a container has just the right touch with yellow, green and brown as decoration and twisting tendrils that echo the shape of the twigs. You could equally well use a plain glass container or a cream or white undecorated jug.

If you want to use the twigs for another arrangement after this one has finished dry the ends of the stems and hang the twigs in a warm place for a week or so to dry out thoroughly. A plant of the corkscrew hazel is easy to grow in a garden but very slow to mature sufficiently to provide plenty of branches.

1 *Fill the jug with water and prepare the ends of the twigs if you want them to open into leaf later.*

2 *Group the twigs at one side of the jug. Place daffodils next to the twigs, letting a few flowers fall naturally around twigs.*

Gerbera and gingham bows

Ingredients

8 long-stemmed gerbera
A tall clear glass
  container
3 × 9 inches (22 cm) of
  gingham ribbon about
  ½ inch (1 cm) wide

Gerbera are spectacular flowers, the texture of their petals and their soft downy stems making them highly individual. Used together in a bunch though they can look a little bland and are seen at their best among other flowers. Their color range is prodigious: from pale cream, many shades of yellow through all the pinks, apricots and peaches to brilliant oranges and reds. Some of the prettiest have a darker eye, such as the ones used here.

Part of the charm of the gerbera is its stem, which is a soft apple green and sometimes quite curvy. Use soft fabric ribbon, not florists' ribbon which is too stiff to tie into small bows. Green gingham would look good on white gerbera or yellow gingham on cream flowers. Other flowers with strong shapely stems could take this treatment too; for example, anemone stems or tulips and tall-stemmed roses. Try using velvet bows for a different effect or mixing brightly colored plain bows through a bunch of mixed freesias. You can add very few bows to one third of the flowers or tie a bow to every stem.

1 *Before putting the gerbera into the glass container and spacing them out well, measure 3 lengths of ribbon.*

2 *Choose the ribbon color to compliment the flowers you have.*

3 *Tie a piece of ribbon to each of three stems.*

4 *Make a small neat bow about 6 inches (15 cm) away from the flower head.*

Clashing colors and colorful tinware

Ingredients

1 large brightly enameled
   metal pot
2 small brightly enameled
   metal pots
A large assortment of
   flowers in brilliant and
   clashing colors; for
   example, marigolds,
   sweet peas and pinks

Brightly decorated Eastern tinware was the starting point for this brilliant mix of clashing colors. You need to approach this arrangement boldly to mix a range of vivid, contrasting colors on a large scale. If you are successful, the result will be stunning. This kind of arrangement is best done in high summer when the choice of flowers is wide-ranging and supply plentiful. If you do not have your own source of suitable varieties, a good flower shop should be able to provide an inspiring collection of blooms.

The small pots are arranged in the same way as the large one. A single container would look fine on its own, but obviously a group arrangement makes a bigger impact. Ensure that all flowers you use have been well conditioned; try using one of the products designed to prolong cut flowers in water.

Work from the viewpoint of the final arrangement (ie, from the front) and do not worry too much about the back. To show off the brilliant colors and varied shapes of your flowers, choose a simple background.

1 *Choose containers in very strong colors. Let their decoration inspire your choice of flowers.*

2 *Fill containers with water. Working from the front edge, begin with two or three large flowers resting against the rim.*

3 *Add the next layer behind the first, mixing colors. Add another layer behind the second, using slightly taller flowers.*

4 *Continue until the container is full and well shaped.*

ANEMONES WITH A PAPER FRILL

Ingredients

A clear glass container
40 blooms of anemones
3 sheets of tissue paper
and matching ribbon

Anemones come in rich glowing colors: red, blue, purple, mauve and white. This brilliant cerise pink is quite a difficult color to use though the soft velvety quality of the anemone petals and stamens stops one stage short of being brash or crude.

The paper collar echoes the green ruff round each flower and softens the brilliant color into something more gentle. This idea would make a superb present to take to someone and it needs no arranging once it has been received. Remember to trim any excess paper away from the stems so that the bunch can simply be dropped into a container of water.

Clear glass marbles are very useful accessories. Their weight makes them perfect for keeping tall thin containers balanced when top heavy flowers are put inside and they can be used to hold stems in place when it is critical to have a flower in exactly the right position. Thin tissue paper works best for this idea and it is available in a good range of colors. A similar idea to this is to cut a white or colored paper doiley, pinning or glueing it into a cone to make a collar round the flower bunch.

1 *Prepare flowers by trimming to even lengths, stripping excess leaves. Bunch flowers together.*

2 *With three sheets of paper together cut rough triangles all along one long edge.*

3 *Move paper so that triangles no longer correspond. Wrap flowers in paper and tie with ribbon just below triangles.*

4 *Cut away excess paper below ribbon to leave stems free to stand in water. Pull back paper frill to frame the flowers.*

Marrows and Melons

Ingredients
1 round melon
A small vegetable
   marrow
A small bunch of mixed
   marigolds
A small bunch of mixed
   nasturtiums

Marrows, squashes, pumpkins and melons all make perfect containers for quick flower arrangements. Naturally waterproof they simply need to be hollowed out to be filled with water or wet florist foam. Their colors and shapes have a natural affinity with late-summer garden flowers and work best filled with very simple bunches of one variety of flower.

Try using a golden yellow melon with brilliant yellow or orange marigolds or coreopsis. The effect is like a patch of sunshine. A group of two or three different-shaped containers with a mix of flower types looks stunning arranged indoors, and one simple globe-shaped squash brimming with yellow centered white daisies or clashing nasturtiums turns an alfresco meal into a special event. It might seem wasteful to use fruit and vegetables in this way, but the flesh of the marrow or melon can be used for a meal before the shell is used as a container. You must leave a reasonable thickness of flesh on the skin however to be sure that the container stays rigid and watertight, and skim just the smallest amount off the base to make it stand steady without leaking. Stand the fruit on a tiny disk of foil to be sure not to stain the furniture below it. A dry-fleshed pumpkin or squash vase will last several days filled with flowers; melons may not last quite as long, but both will probably outlive the flowers inside them. Try using an arrangement like this on a summer dinner table and complement it with a green-salad mixed·with edible nasturtium and marigold petals.

1 *Skim off a small amount of skin at base to make melon stand steady. Slice off a lid, scoop out seeds and flesh.*

2 *Make marigolds into a bunch in your hand, cut stems to same length and put marigolds into the melon.*

3 *The nasturtiums in the long marrow will need to be put in place one or two at a time.*

A POSY OF ROSES

Ingredients
A small basket
A waterproof container
   to fit inside the basket
45 stems miniature roses
15 sprigs sweet bay leaves
Rubber bands

Making a small and manageable posy of flowers is very quick and simple. Most people have at some time picked a bunch of flowers from the garden or hedgerow and hastily made a posy to fit the hand. The technique works well for both simple flowers and very sophisticated ones. Posies are often chosen as gifts or for bridesmaids to carry at weddings.

A century or more ago posies made from neat concentric circles of different flowers were extremely popular. In times when plague and infectious diseases were common, tiny posies of flowers, known as 'tussy mussies', were carried to ward off germs. It is a lovely idea to include scented flowers in a posy. If possible, the foliage should be scented too. Many herbs make perfect ingredients for posies; try using, rue, mint, thyme, rosemary, bay, hyssop and sage.

This posy is made from tightly-packed miniature roses surrounded by a green edging of sprigs of sweet bay leaves. When it is made it can stand in a small jug or cup, a glass or vase, or it can be put inside a water-filled container in a basket. The basket shown here is coarse, twiggy and heartshaped.

1 Trim the lower leaves from the bay sprigs, leaving about 4 to 6 leaves on each sprig.

2 Take the roses and build them into a round posy which fits into the hand.

3 Secure roses with a rubber band. Add bay leaves, working round posy. When complete, secure with band.

4 Trim off all the stems neatly and place the bunch in water, inside the basket.

INDEX